Leaping Learners
Education, LLC

For more information and resources visit us at:
www.leapinglearnersed.com

©Sean Bulger

Published by Leaping Learners, LLC, Verona, NJ 07044 . All rights reserved. Reproduction in whole or inpart without written permission of the publisher is prohibited.

Every attempt has been made to credit each photo. Please contact us if there has been an error and we will resolve the issue.

Photo Credits
Yellow cheese, © Brent Hofacker/stock.adobe.com

All design by Sean Bulger
All other pictures by Sean Bulger or royalty free from Pixabay.com

ISBN
978-1-948569-09-5

Dear Parents and Guardians,

Thank you for purchasing a *Clayton Teaches About* series book! After teaching students from kindergarten to second grade for more than seven years, I became frustrated by the lack of engaging books my students could read independently. To help my students engage with nonfiction topics, my wife and I decided to write nonfiction books for children. We hope to inspire young children to learn about the natural world.

Here at Leaping Learners Education, LLC, we have three main goals:

1. Spark young readers' curiosity about the natural world
2. Develop critical independent reading skills at an early age
3. Develop reading comprehension skills before and after reading

We hope your child enjoys learning with Clayton. If you or your children are interested in a topic we have not written about yet, send us an email with your topic, and maybe your book will be next!

                              Thank you,

                              Sean Bulger, Ed.M

www.leapinglearnersed.com

Reading Suggestions:

Before reading this book, encourage your children to do a "picture walk" where they skim through the book looking the pictures to help them think about what they already know about the topic. Thinking back about what they already know helps children to get excited about learning more facts and begin reading with some confidence.

Preview any new vocabulary words with your child. Have your child use the phrase in their own words to see if they understand the definition.

After previewing the book, encourage your child to read the book independently more than once. After they have finished reading, encourage them to complete the reading comprehension exercises at the end of the book to strengthen their reading skills!

This book is best for ages 5-6

but. . .
Please be mindful that reading levels are a guide and vary depending on a child's skills and needs.

Yellow

Written by Sean Bulger

Hi! My name is Clayton. As you can see... I am a crayon! Come and learn about the color yellow with me.

There is corn. The corn is **yellow**.

There is a chick. The chick is **yellow**.

There is cheese. The cheese is **yellow**.

There are bananas. The bananas are **yellow**.

There is a bus. The bus is **yellow**.

There is butter. The butter is **yellow**.

There is a sunflower. The sunflower is **yellow**.

There is the sun. The sun is **yellow**.

There is a sponge. The sponge is **yellow**.

There are lemons. The lemons are yellow.

Do you know anything else that is yellow? Draw it!

There is a _____.
The _____ is yellow.

Do you know anything else that is yellow? Draw it!

There is a _____.
The _____ is yellow.

Find and circle the word "there"

am

there

am

See

the

there

me We

am

there them

the

Find and circle the word "just"

are   just   am
            See
I   The
            are
am   We
just See
            am
did   The
      I   just